Fossils

by Becky Olien

Consultant:
Francesca Pozzi, Research Associate
Center for International Earth Science Information Network
Columbia University

Bridgestone Books
an imprint of Capstone Press
Mankato, Minnesota

Bridgestone Books are published by Capstone Press,
151 Good Counsel Drive, P.O. Box 669, Mankato, Minnesota 56002.
www.capstonepress.com

Library of Congress Cataloging-in-Publication Data
Olien, Rebecca.
    Fossils/by Becky Olien.
    p. cm.—(The Bridgestone science library)
    Includes bibliographical references and index.
    ISBN 0-7368-0951-1
    1. Fossils—Juvenile literature. [1. Fossils.] I. Title. II. Series.
QE714.5 .O45 2002
560—dc21

                                                        00-012593

Summary: Discusses types of fossils and what scientists can learn from them; also gives
    information on fossil fuels.

Editorial Credits
Rebecca Glaser, editor; Karen Risch, product planning editor; Linda Clavel, designer
    and illustrator; Jeff Anderson, photo researcher

Photo Credits
Digital Wisdom, globe images
James P. Rowan, 6, 20
Jana R. Jirak/Root Resources, 8
Jeff Foott/TOM STACK & ASSOCIATES, 10
Jeff Daly/Photo Agora, 14
Mary A. Root/Root Resources, cover, 1
Rick Brady/Pictor, 18
Tom Till, 4, 12
Visuals Unlimited/Ken Lucas, 16

Cover Photo: Ammonite fossil, Alberta, Canada

  2 3 4 5 6 08 07 06 05 04

Table of Contents

Clues about the Past

Fossils are preserved remains of plants and animals. Most fossils are millions of years old.

Most fossils are found in sedimentary rock. This type of rock once was sand or mud. Dead plants and animals were buried in the sand or mud. The sand and mud then turned into rock and preserved the plants and animals as fossils.

Paleontologists study fossils to find clues about the past. They learn what kinds of plants and animals lived long ago. They learn how animals lived and became extinct.

Scientists study fossils to learn about changes in the land. The same fossils found in South America and Africa show that the continents once may have been joined. Fossils of animals that lived in warm places have been found in Antarctica. The climate may have been warm on this continent long ago. Fossils prove that Earth has gone through many changes.

This palm fossil and fish fossil were found in the Green River Formation in Wyoming.

How Fossils Form

Most plants and animals do not become fossils. Other animals often eat plants and animals when they die. Dead animals and plants rot if they are not eaten. Sun, wind, and rain help break down the animals and plants.

Fossils form only in certain conditions. Minerals replace plant and animal remains before they rot. This process happens when the remains are buried quickly. The remains turn to stone or make an imprint in the rock.

Forces of nature bury plants and animals quickly. Floods wash sand over dead bodies. Volcanoes cover creatures with ash and lava. Earthquakes cause landslides that bury plants and animals in mud.

Many fossils are tiny ocean plants or animals. They sink to the ocean floor when they die. Cold water keeps dead plants and animals from rotting. The bodies slowly change into fossils.

Trilobites are now extinct. Fossils of these ocean animals show that they lived about 540 million years ago.

Types of Fossils

Three types of fossils exist on Earth. They are body fossils, imprint fossils, and trace fossils.

Body fossils are bones, teeth, and eggs. Bones show the shape and size of animals. Teeth give clues about how and what animals ate. Egg fossils help scientists learn how young animals grew.

Imprint fossils can be mold or cast fossils. Mold fossils are imprints of plants, bones, and shells in rock. Cast fossils are mold fossils filled with hardened minerals. Cast fossils look like the bone or shell they replaced. Imprint fossils give important clues to how ancient plants and animals looked.

Trace fossils are signs an animal leaves behind. Footprints are the most common trace fossils. Scientists can figure out an animal's size, weight, and speed from its footprints. Other trace fossils include nests, claw marks, and animal tunnels. Paleontologists study trace fossils to learn how animals lived.

Many body fossils of dinosaurs can be seen at Dinosaur National Monument Park in Utah and Colorado.

Plant Fossils

The oldest fossils are plant fossils. Algae were the first plants to appear on Earth about two billion years ago. Cold ocean water helped turn algae into fossils. Algae fossils help scientists study the history of plants on Earth.

The first land plants began growing about 400 million years ago. They were club mosses, horsetails, and ferns. These plants grew when dinosaurs were alive. Scientists find imprint fossils of these plants in rock deep underground.

Fossil trees are petrified, or turned into stone. Minerals slowly replaced the wood in the trees to form these fossils. The trees changed into colorful stone. The Petrified Forest National Park in Arizona has many petrified trees.

Many species of ancient plants are alive today. A species that has not changed over time is called a living fossil. The ginkgo tree is a living fossil. It has not changed for 150 million years.

Visitors to Petrified Forest National Park in Arizona can see the colorful stone of petrified logs.

What Is a Paleontologist?

Paleontologists study fossils to learn about plants and animals of the past. They travel to sites where fossils are found. They work carefully to dig fossils out of the ground. Paleontologists study fossils in laboratories. They run tests to find the fossils' age. Each discovery adds clues about what Earth was like in the past.

Dinosaur Fossils

Dinosaur fossils are the largest fossils on Earth. Scientists began finding dinosaur fossils in the early 1800s. At first, scientists thought the bones were from living animal species.

Paleontologists learned that the bones were from huge reptiles. Scientists now know that dinosaurs lived on Earth for about 150 million years. These animals died out long before humans lived. In 1990, Susan Hendrickson discovered a well-preserved Tyrannosaurus rex skeleton in South Dakota. It was the most complete skeleton ever found of this large, meat-eating dinosaur.

Scientists study fossils to discover why dinosaurs became extinct about 65 million years ago. Some scientists think a giant meteorite fell to Earth. The meteorite sent dust into the air when it crashed into Earth. The dust blocked out sunlight so the planet became cooler. Most plants and animals could not survive without sunlight.

The dinosaur footprints at the bottom of the photograph are some of the best preserved tracks in North America.

Fun Fact

Fossils of dragonflies with 28-inch (71-centimeter) wingspans have been found.

Small Animal Fossils

Most fossils are from animals that are smaller than dinosaurs. The fossils give scientists clues about these early animals.

The oldest animal fossils are from soft-bodied worms and jellyfish. These fossils are rare because these animals do not have bones or shells.

Many shelled animals lived in large groups. Their fossils made coral reefs and limestone rock layers that are 500 million years old.

The first fish fossils also are about 500 million years old. Fish fossils tell scientists that these fish did not have a backbone, teeth, or jaws. Fish with bones and teeth appeared on Earth about 150 million years later. Some of these fish had fins that helped them move on land.

Most insect remains rotted too quickly to become fossils. Rare insect fossils have been found in hardened tree sap and in shale. These finds show that insects were alive 365 million years ago.

Some insect fossils are preserved in hardened tree sap that has turned to amber.

Famous Fossil Finds

People have discovered fossils throughout the world. Paleontologists work together to discover how life on Earth has changed. Each new fossil gives scientists more clues about how Earth has changed over time.

The Burgess Shale is an important fossil site in British Columbia, Canada. Charles Walcott discovered this area in 1909. The Burgess Shale contains many fossils of creatures without bones. These creatures usually rot before fossils can form.

In 1924, Noel Odell found fossils of shelled ocean animals on Mount Everest. These fossils showed that Mount Everest once was under the ocean.

In 1990, scientists found dinosaur fossils near the South Pole. They had found similar types of fossils in Asia and South Africa. The locations of these fossils show that Earth's continents have moved over time.

Anomalocaris is the largest fossil found in the Burgess Shale. This photograph shows one of the undersea predator's claws.

Fossil Fuels

People burn fossil fuels for heat and electricity. Coal, oil, and natural gas are fossil fuels. They formed from plants and animals that lived on Earth millions of years ago.

Coal comes from plants that lived about 300 million years ago. The plants grew in swamps. Muddy soil covered the plants when they died. The plants could not rot without air. They turned into a thick, black liquid. The liquid became hard over time. Today, coal lies far below Earth's surface. Workers dig mines underground to find and remove coal.

Oil and natural gas are made mostly from the remains of plankton. These tiny plants and animals were buried under the ocean floor. After millions of years, water and rock pressed the fossils into oil and natural gas. These fuels move underground through holes in rocks. People build large machines called rigs to bring oil and natural gas to Earth's surface.

People burn coal for energy. Coal takes 300 million years to form.

Conserving Fossil Fuels

Fossil fuels will not last forever. Coal and oil take millions of years to form. People need to conserve their use of fossil fuels. Fossil fuels will last longer if people use less energy or find new energy sources.

Cars burn a lot of fuel. Taking buses or subways to work and school helps save gasoline. People conserve fuel by walking or riding bikes instead of driving cars.

Power companies burn fossil fuels to create electricity. People need electricity to heat, cool, and light their homes. People can save electricity by turning off lights and appliances when they are not in use.

People save fossil fuels by learning different ways to use energy. People are inventing new cars and machines that use less energy. They also are finding new energy sources. Solar power, wind power, and nuclear power can provide energy without burning fossil fuels.

Taking buses or sharing rides helps save fossil fuels.

Hands On: Digging for Bones

Bone fossils usually are broken. Paleontologists try to fit the pieces together.

What You Need

Newspaper
Dishpan full of sand
Six bone-shaped dog biscuits
Small shovels
Buckets
Small paint brushes
White glue

What You Do

1. Cover a table or counter with newspaper.
2. Place the dishpan full of sand on the newspaper.
3. Break the dog biscuits into three or four pieces.
4. Bury the pieces in the dishpan full of sand.
5. Carefully dig through the sand to find the bone pieces. Put the sand you dig up in the buckets.
6. Use the paint brushes to brush the sand off the bones.
7. Place the bone pieces onto the newspaper.
8. See how many bones you can fit back together.
9. Glue the bones together with white glue.

Words to Know

algae (AL-jee)—small plants without roots or stems that grow in water or on damp surfaces

amber (AM-bur)—a yellowish brown substance formed from fossilized tree sap; some insect fossils are preserved in amber.

extinct (ek-STINGKT)—no longer living anywhere in the world

mineral (MIN-ur-uhl)—a substance found in nature

nuclear power (NOO-klee-ur POU-ur)—power created by splitting atoms; atoms are the smallest part of a substance.

sedimentary rock (sed-uh-MEN-tuh-ree ROK)—rock made of pressed layers of rock, sand, and dirt

shale (SHAYL)—rock formed from hardened mud

solar power (SOH-lur POU-ur)—energy from the sun that can be used for heating and electricity

species (SPEE-sheez)—a group of plants or animals that share common characteristics

Read More

Burton, Jane, and Kim Taylor. *The Nature and Science of Fossils.* Exploring the Science of Nature. Milwaukee: Gareth Stevens Publishing, 1999.

Gish, Melissa, and Nancy J. Shaw. *Fossils.* Let's Investigate. Mankato, Minn.: Creative Education, 2000.

Robinson, Fay. *A Dinosaur Named Sue: The Find of the Century.* Hello Reader! New York: Scholastic, 1999.

Useful Addresses

Vancouver Paleontological Society
Centrepoint Post Office
PO Box 19653
Vancouver, BC V5T 4E7
Canada

Wyoming Dinosaur Center
110 Carter Ranch Road
P.O. Box 868
Thermopolis, WY 82443

Internet Sites

Do you want to find out more about fossils?
Here's how:
1) Go to *http://www.facthound.com*
2) Type in the **Book ID** number: **0736809511**
3) Click on **FETCH IT.**

Index